T5-AGC-244

Bat Boy and Other Strange Creatures

Debra Hess

SCHOLASTIC INC.

New York Toronto London Auckland Sydney
Mexico City New Delhi Hong Kong Buenos Aires

Cover Photo
© 2003 American Media

Copyright © 2004 by Scholastic Inc.
All rights reserved. Published by Scholastic Inc.
Printed in the U.S.A.

ISBN 0-439-68256-8

SCHOLASTIC, READ 180, and associated logos and designs are trademarks and/or registered trademarks of Scholastic Inc.

LEXILE is a registered trademark of MetaMetrics, Inc.

3   4   5   6   7   8   9   10   23   12 11 10 09 08

Contents

Introduction

There are monsters in the movies. There are **creatures** in cartoons. There are **beasts** in books. But are any of them real?

Bat Boy

Some of them *are* real.

But some are fake. People say they've seen them. But they've really made them up!

Sea Squirt

Get ready to learn about six monsters. Which ones are real? Which are fake?

Roadrunner

See if *you* can guess.

Giant Squid

Loch Ness Monster

Ape Man

creatures things that are living
beasts monsters

It is half-bat and half-boy.
And it only eats bugs!

1

Bat Boy

What People Say

A **scientist** named Ron Dillon was in a dark cave. He heard a strange sound. Then he saw a four-year-old boy. The boy was hiding in a corner of the cave!

The boy was two feet tall. He weighed only 19 pounds. He had huge orange eyes. He had pointed ears.

scientist a person who studies nature

Ron Dillon called him Bat Boy. Ron took Bat Boy to a hospital. Doctors said he was fine. But he would only eat bugs.

Then Bat Boy ran away!

Lots of people say they have seen Bat Boy. One man even said he caught Bat Boy. He put Bat Boy in his garage. But then Bat Boy ran away. No one has ever caught him again. Why?

The Truth

Bat Boy is . . . *fake.*

More About Bat Boy

Bat Boy was made up by a writer. The writer works for the *Weekly World News.* The *News* prints lots of fake stories.

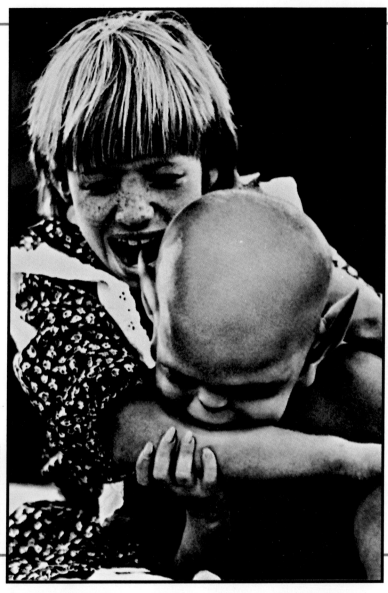

The *Weekly World News* printed this fake photo of Bat Boy biting a girl. The *News* also reported that Bat Boy bit the U.S. Vice President!

When it's young, it eats its own brain.
And it never even misses it!

2

Sea Squirt

What People Say

Like most creatures, the sea squirt is born with a brain. But it needs that brain for only one thing. The brain helps it find a home.

The young sea squirt swims through the sea. It tries to find something to grab onto. It could grab a rock, a piece of

These sea squirts have found a home on coral. Now all they do is suck water with food in it into one hole, and then squirt it out the other hole!

coral, or even a boat. The young squirt grabs onto its new home. Then it stays there the rest of its life!

The sea squirt's brain has done its job. It isn't needed anymore. So the sea squirt does something really strange. It eats its own brain!

coral stuff that grows underwater and is made of the skeletons of tiny sea creatures

The Truth

The sea squirt is . . . *real*.

More About the Sea Squirt

The sea squirt is famous for eating its brain. It's also famous for one other thing. It squirts!

The sea squirt has two holes in its body. It sucks water into one hole. The water has tiny bits of food in it. The sea squirt soaks up the food. Then it squirts the water out its other hole.

When does the sea squirt eat its brain?

This bird can hardly fly. But it runs fast.
And it eats its own babies.

3

Roadrunner

What People Say

There's a really weird bird. It lives in the southwestern part of the United States. The bird can fly. But it can't fly very well. It can fly for only a few seconds. Then it crashes to the ground.

So how does this bird get around? It runs! In fact, it runs more than it flies.

That's why it's called a roadrunner.

The roadrunner is fast. It can run faster than 20 miles per hour. It's so fast it can catch a rattlesnake. First it kills the snake by hitting its head against the ground. Then it eats the snake!

The Truth

The Roadrunner is . . . *real.*

More About the Roadrunner

The roadrunner is a cuckoo. That's a kind of bird that gets its energy from the sun. During the day, it saves up energy in a patch on its back. At night, it uses that energy to get around.

Besides snakes, the roadrunner eats

This lizard didn't have a chance! The roadrunner is so fast that it can catch a hummingbird or dragonfly in midair.

mice and other birds. And sometimes it eats its own babies! But the roadrunner can't eat a whole animal at once. So it eats part of it. The rest hangs from its beak. That way the roadrunner knows where its next meal is coming from!

It's not an ape. It's not a man.
It's . . . the Ape Man!

Ape Man

What People Say

The Ape Man is a giant hairy beast. It lives in forests. People all over the world have seen it. Some people call it Big Foot. Others have named it Sasquatch. And some people call it the Yeti.

No one has ever caught an Ape Man. But once, someone found a **scalp**. A

scalp the skin and hair on a human or animal's head

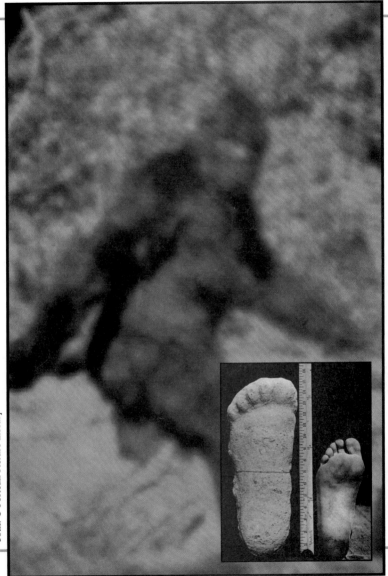

In 1967, a man in California said he filmed the Ape Man. The big photo is from his film. *Bottom right*: Some people say this is Bigfoot's footprint. It's 16 inches long. (The human footprint next to it is 11 inches long.) Do you think the film and footprint are real?

scalp is the skin and hair on a human or animal's head. Some people said that this scalp did not come from a human or a normal animal. They said it came from the head of an Ape Man!

The Truth

The Ape Man is most likely . . . *fake.*

But what about that scalp? Scientists say it came from a goat!

More About the Ape Man

Sir Edmund Hillary was a famous mountain climber. He had heard stories about the Ape Man. He led people on a hunt to find one. They looked for 10 months. But they didn't find an Ape Man!

There's one dinosaur left.
It's living in a lake in Scotland.

5

Loch Ness Monster

What People Say

A monster swims in a lake in a country called Scotland. The lake is called Loch Ness. So the monster is called the Loch Ness Monster. Some people call it Nessie for short.

Nessie has a long neck and a head like a snake. It has fins. It also has humps on its back. People say it's a dinosaur.

The Loch Ness Monster was first seen about a thousand years ago. Since then, hundreds of people have spotted it.

The Truth

Nessie is most likely . . . *fake.*

More About the Loch Ness Monster

Some people say they've taken pictures of Nessie. But most of the pictures are fake. Or they're really fuzzy or dark. They're not **proof** that Nessie is real.

Do you think it's possible that a dinosaur still lives on Earth? Why?

proof facts that show that something is true

The big photo was taken by a doctor in 1934. He said it was Nessie. But 60 years later, people found out it wasn't. The doctor had probably taken a photo of a toy dinosaur! *Bottom left*: In 1969, a Nessie-hunter took a submarine deep into Loch Ness but didn't find the beast.

Is there a monster with ten arms living at the bottom of the sea?

Giant Squid

What People Say

There's a monster that lives at the bottom of the ocean. People call it the giant squid. It is about 60 feet long. That's about twice as long as a school bus. The squid weighs 2,000 pounds. Each of its eyes is the size of a human head.

The giant squid eats fish, crabs, and

People have talked about the giant squid for hundreds of years. In the 1800s, an artist made this picture of a giant squid attacking a ship.

even sharks. It catches animals with the suckers on its two long **tentacles**. Then it squeezes the animals tight with its eight other arms. Each arm has a sharp, strong beak that can rip animals apart.

This scary monster may even have killed a person. But only a few people have run into one.

The giant squid was last seen off the coast of New Zealand.

The Truth

The giant squid is . . . *real.*

More About the Giant Squid

More than 200 dead giant squids have washed up on beaches. But these

tentacles long, rope-like arms

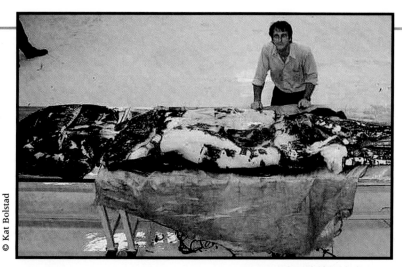

© Kat Bolstad

This giant squid was caught near New Zealand. It is about 20 feet long. When it's fully grown, it could be twice that size. "If you fell in the water next to it, you would be in big trouble," one scientist said.

creatures live so deep in the ocean that no one had ever seen a live one.

Then, in 2003, fishers on a boat in New Zealand caught a live one! Scientists said it could grow to be bigger than a whale! "You would not want to meet this in the water," said one scientist.

Glossary

beasts *(noun)* monsters

coral *(noun)* stuff that grows underwater and is made of the skeletons of tiny sea creatures

creatures *(noun)* things that are living

proof *(noun)* facts that show that something is true

scalp *(noun)* the skin and hair on a human or animal's head

scientist *(noun)* a person who studies nature *(related word: science)*

tentacles *(noun)* long, rope-like arms